Jessie's World

"The New Baby"

by D.L. Patillo

BOOKSIDE Press

Jessie's World: "The New Baby" © 2022 D. L. Patillo

All rights reserved. No part of this publication may be reproduced, distributed, or transmitted in any form or by any means, including photocopying, recording, or other electronic or mechanical methods, without the prior written permission of the publisher, except in the case brief quotations embodied in critical reviews and other noncommercial uses permitted by copyright law.

ISBN:
Paperback   978-1-990695-71-1
Hardback   978-1-990695-73-5
E-book   978-1-990695-72-8

The views expressed in this book are solely those of the author and do not necessarily reflect the views of the publisher, and the publisher hereby disclaims any responsibility for them.

BOOKSIDE Press

BookSide Press
877-741-8091
www.booksidepress.com
orders@booksidepress.com

Jessie is very excited about the new bicycle his dad promised him for his birthday. He imagined riding the blue racing bicycle with training wheels and wearing his helmet for safety. He wanted to race his bike and honk his horn.

Jessie sat up in his bed very happy and excited! "Today is my birthday!" he said. Jessie is turning four today, but even more special than that, Jessie's mommy is coming home soon with the new baby.

Jessie had to keep a promise to his dad so he could get the bicycle. Jessie promised his dad he would be obedient in school and at home and that he would keep his room tidy. His dad said that would make him a big boy. Jessie had been good most of the time, so he was certain his dad was going to get his bicycle today!

Jessie sat patiently in the kitchen while his dad cooked him breakfast. "Good morning, Daddy", he said with a smile. His dad smiled back, "Hi Big Fella". "Dad, I'm up and downstairs and Rachel did not have to help me", he said with pride. His sister Rachel always has to get Jessie up for breakfast. "I'm a big boy, aren't I?" Jessie asked. "Yes, Jessie, that is what big boys do".

"Am I ready for my bicycle now?" Jessie inquired. "Of course, you are son", dad replied. "But I don't know if we will be able to get it before Mommy comes home with the baby". "Well," said Jessie, "If Mommy brings my little brother home by this afternoon, it will still be my birthday, so it will be fine". "Ok Jessie, but there is no guarantee Mommy and the baby will be home today and we don't know if it is a girl or a boy." dad said with a smile.

Jessie liked the idea of having a brother to play with. He was even more excited about all of the things he could do with a baby brother. They could play with trucks and games together. "I'm going to be a big brother now," he thought to himself. Jessie had his heart set on a brother so much so he could not imagine the baby would be a girl at all.

Later that morning, Jessie wondered if his mommy was ready to come home. His dad had already left for the hospital. But before he left, he talked to Jessie about helping his mommy more around the house. Jessie wanted to do his part now that he was a big boy. He wondered, "What would I have to do?" He asked his sister. And she told him she always had to keep her room clean and pick up her toys. "Oh" she said, "and you know big boys no longer take naps". Rachel always liked picking on her little brother because of all the attention he got from their parents.

"No more naps!", he said with great surprise. That was his favorite time with his mom. He always got a hug and a kiss before he took a nap. His mommy would give him a snack when he woke up. Jessie really felt sad about what his sister had told him.

The next day mommy and the baby were due to arrive home. It was after Jessie's birthday and he had forgotten all about the bicycle. All day he had been thinking about his new brother coming home. His room was clean and he had taken out some of his baby toys for his little brother.

Just then, he heard the car pull up in the driveway and then the front door opening. It was his mommy, daddy and the new baby. His daddy called out, "Rachel, Jessie we're home!".

Jessie ran down the stairs so fast, he could barely stop! "Hey, slow down son", said dad. Jessie was so excited that the baby had finally arrived. He thought, "I have a new baby brother to play with". He did not have to worry about his sister Rachel spending time with him. "Let me see him" "Pleaseee, Mommy can I see him now!", Jessie said with much excitement.

Mommy opened the blanket and to Jessie's surprise the baby was wearing pink clothing. Jessie thought to himself, "Mommy always says girls wear pink and boys wear blue. He wondered why his new little brother was wearing pink. Jessie was so certain he was having a baby brother he could not believe it could be a baby girl.

Jessie asked his mother, "Did you give him a name yet? Why is he wearing pink? Did the hospital run out of boy clothes?" Jessie was so certain that the baby was a boy, but was just wearing the wrong color clothes. Mommy laughed. She knew how much he wanted a brother. "No sweetheart, this is your baby sister and yes we have given her a name, it is Kayla". "The baby is wearing pink, because girls wear pink".

"A GIRL!!" He said. He paused a moment. What would he do with a girl baby? He thought. He did not have any toys for a girl. Mom had answered all of Jessie's questions, but there had to be some way he could get a baby brother.

He thought of an idea, and with a feeling of happiness, he asked his mom, "Mommy, can't we just take her back and get a brother baby?". "Did you keep the receipt?" Mom was surprised at what he said. Rachel and dad looked away to hide their laughter, but mom understood Jessie's feelings of loneliness. His mom just smiled and said, "No, sweetheart, we can't do that! She belongs to us". "But soon you will grow to love her and take care of her". Jessie was still very sad. He had not planned anything for a sister, only a brother. What would he do with a sister?

Jessie woke up from his afternoon nap, and found Rachel reading a book in her room. "Rachel, how do I play with a baby sister? and what do they like to do?" Jessie asked. Rachel explained, "Well babies don't do much at first". "They cry, sleep, eat and they get their diapers changed."

"I just hope I don't have to babysit", she said. Jessie decided to go ask his father.

"Daddy", said Jessie, "What can a baby girl do?" "What do you mean son?", his father said. "Can I play with her?" said Jessie. "Well," said his dad. "She can't do much right now because she is too small"."But soon you will be able to help her walk and talk". "Hey! ask your mother if you can help her with the baby now".

Jessie watched as his mommy fed Kayla. Jessie was curious because, he had never been around a small baby before. "Mommy, what do you do with a girl baby?" he asked, "Well, she has to be fed and her diaper changed, bathe her, and put her down for nap and give her plenty of love, just like I did with you and Rachel." she said, "But you are a big boy, tying your shoes and putting on your own clothes all by yourself".

Jessie remembered what Rachel had said about taking naps. "Mommy, do big boys still take naps?", asked Jessie. "ummm", his mom replied, "Well do you still take naps at school", she asked. Jessie responded, "YES!". "Well", said mommy, "I guess you can take them a little while longer at home, BUT big boys don't take naps like babies".

Jessie did not want to be a baby, but he missed his mom, naptime and getting snacks when he got up. This made him very sad. His mommy sensed he was sad. She wanted to cheer him up. She had an idea. "Sweetie", she said, "Since Kayla is such a formal name, do you want to give her your own special nickname?" Jessie was very happy, but what could he name her?

He remembered the little girl from school. She was fun to play with. "Can we name her Kay Kay?" Jessie said. "That's my friend's name at school." "Sure", said mom. "Let's put her down for her nap". Jessie's mom hugged and kissed the baby. Then she remembered her second baby. She picked Jessie up and gave him the biggest hug and kiss ever. Jessie thought to himself, I think I can share my mommy with a baby sister.

The End

www.ingramcontent.com/pod-product-compliance
Lightning Source LLC
LaVergne TN
LVHW070437080526
838202LV00036B/2836